He Tells Tales of Meroe
Poems for the Petrie Museum

كأنّما يروي عن مروي
قصائد لمتحف "بيتري" في لندن

Al-Saddiq Al-Raddi holds limestone frog from Meroe

He Tells Tales of Meroe
Poems for the Petrie Museum
كأنّما يروي عن مروي
قصائد لمتحف "بيتري" في لندن

by Al-Saddiq Al-Raddi
الصَّادق الرضي

Translated by Sarah Maguire and Mark Ford
with Rashid Elsheikh, Atef Alshaer and Hafiz Kheir

With an Introduction by Professor Stephen Quirke
and photographs by Crispin Hughes

Poems © Al-Saddiq Al-Raddi
Petrie Poems translations © Sarah Maguire and Rashid Elsheikh
'Poem of the Nile' translation © Mark Ford and Hafiz Kheir
Writing in the Shadow of Archaeology © Al-Saddiq Al-Raddi
Introduction translation © Atef Ashaer

Al-Saddiq Al-Raddi and the Sudanese Archaeological Collections
at the Petrie Museum, UCL © Stephen Quirke

'Stained with the Tincture of History': A Poet in the Museum © Sarah Maguire

Photographs © Crispin Hughes

ISBN: 978-0-9575511-9-0

First published 2015 by
The Poetry Translation Centre
Free Word Centre
60 Farringdon Road
London EC1R 3GA

www.poetrytranslation.org

Supported by Arts Council England

British Library Cataloguing-in-Publication Data.
A catalogue record for this book is available from the British Library

Designed in Rialto by Libanus Press Ltd
Cover design: North Kuras, Exploded View
Printed in the UK by Rubine Press
on acid-free paper sourced from mills with
FSC chain of custody certification

Contents

Writing in the Shadow of Archaeology *Al-Saddiq Al-Raddi*	7
Al-Saddiq Al-Raddi and the Sudanese Archaeological Collections at the Petrie Museum, UCL *Professor Stephen Quirke*	13
'Stained with the Tincture of History': A Poet in the Museum *Sarah Maguire*	16

POEMS FOR THE PETRIE MUSEUM
Translated by Sarah Maguire and Rashid Elsheikh

The Key of Life	21
Traces of an Unknown Woman	25
They Think I Am a King: Yes I Am the King	29
He Tells Tales of Meroe	33
Schism	35
Killing Time	39
A Monkey Following a Monkey	41
The Golden Scarab Necklace	47
Poem of the Nile *Translated by Mark Ford and Hafiz Kheir*	53
Acknowledgements	61
Biographies	62

أن تكتب على ضوء العراقة

الصّادق الرضي

"قصيدة النيل" ربما كانت هي مفتاح علاقتي بمتحف "بيتري" في لندن، القصيدة كتبت في ثمانينيات القرن المنصرم، نشرت في كتابي الشعري الأول، صدر في الخرطوم، في طبعته الأولى 1996م، وهي ضمن مجموعة القصائد الأولى التي ترجمت من العربية للإنجليزية، بواسطة مركز ترجمة الشعر في لندن، تمهيدا لمشاركتي في "الجولة الأولى لشعراء العالم بالمملكة المتحدة- أكتوبر 2005م"؛ في زيارتي الثانية للمملكة المتحدة مطلع العام 2006م مشاركا في "مؤتمر الترجمة من العربية للإنجليزية ومن الإنجليزية للعربية" الذي نظمه مجلس الآداب البريطاني على هامش "معرض لندن الدولي للكتاب"- وقتها، نشرت مجلة "لندن ريفيو بوك" القصيدة مترجمة في صفحة كاملة.

قراءة شعرية دعيت لها من "كوفي بوتري" في لندن مارس 2006م، ومناقشة من الجمهور إثر الفراغ من القراءة، إثرها تشرفت بمعرفة Professor Stephen Quirke بروفيسور ستيفان مدير متحف "بيتري" وقتها وإلى وقت قريب، مبدياً إعجابه بـ "قصيدة النيل" ووجه لي دعوة لزيارة المتحف للتعرف على مقتنياته، لبيت الدعوة بعد عدة أيام، حيث أعرب لي عن رغبته في "اقتناء" القصيدة لتضم إلى مقتنيات المتحف الثمينة، أدهشني الأمر وأفرحني، وافقت مبدئيا وأنا لا أعرف كيف سيفعل ذلك؛ ثم غادرت إلى الخرطوم، حين عدت في سبتمبر من ذات العام، أعدّ لنا حفل تدشين لـ "لوحة"- رسمت عليها خريطة السودان بالتركيز على نهر النيل، وعلى جانبيْ النهر، كتب النص باللغتين العربية والإنجليزية، بخط اليد، كان تدشينا أنيقا حضره لفيف من المهتمين والإعلاميين.

في العام 2010م، كنت مدعوا للمشاركة في مهرجان روتردام العالمي للشعر في هولندا، تزامنت تلك الدعوة مع برامج نسقها مركز ترجمة الشعر في لندن مع مهرجانات ومناسبات شعرية عديدة في المملكة المتحدة، الأمر الذي استغرق مني نحو 3 أشهر وتزيد، متجولا بين هولندا وبريطانيا؛ في تلك الأثناء أعدّ متحف "بيتري" في لندن، مناسبة خاصة احتفاء بي- قدمت فيها قراءات شعرية وكانت

Writing in the Shadow of Archaeology

AL-SADDIQ AL-RADDI

Written in the late 1980s and published in my first collection of poetry, 'Poem of the Nile' is perhaps the key to my relationship with the Petrie Museum in London. 'Poem of the Nile' was one of the first of my poems translated into English by the Poetry Translation Centre in preparation for my participation in the PTC's first World Poets' Tour in October 2005. In 2006 'Poem of the Nile' was published in *The London Review of Books* in its entirety.

During my second visit to the UK in the spring of 2006 to take part in a conference on translation between Arabic and English organised by the British Council, I gave a reading at the Poetry Cafe. I was delighted to discover that Professor Stephen Quirke, then Curator at the Petrie Museum, was in the audience. He kindly invited me to the museum to view its Sudanese collections and, when we met there, Stephen asked if 'Poem of the Nile' could be added to the museum's precious acquisitions. Although at the time I didn't understand how this could be possible, when I visited London again that autumn Stephen organised a party at the museum at which a beautiful painting of the Nile had been inscribed with my poem in English and Arabic.

In 2010, during a visit to Europe thanks to an invitation to participate in the Poetry International Festival in Rotterdam, I also visited the UK on behalf of the Poetry Translation Centre where I spent three months taking part in a number of readings and festivals. The highlight of my visit was a wonderful party arranged by the Petrie Museum at which I read several poems, an occasion that cemented my relationship with the staff of the museum, and that between the PTC and the Petrie. I think it was this event that hatched the idea of offering me a residency in the museum, something that became a reality in 2012.

One of the most memorable times at the museum during my resi-

هناك أيضا مساحة رحبة لأسئلة ومداخلات الحضورز؛ في تلك الأمسية توثقت أواصر التواصل مع أسرة "المتحف" و"مركز ترجمة الشعر"، وربما في تلك الأمسية، بدأ التفكير في مشروع "الإقامة الشعرية" الأمر الذي بدأ فعليا في مطلع يوليو 2012م.

اليوم المخصص لعمل فريق التصوير الفوتغرافي بقيادة المبدع "Crispin Hughes" كان يوما مميزا من أيام عملي في المتحف، كانت هناك شابة متطوعة تعمل في المتحف، لا أذكر اسمها الآن- للأسف، قالت لي هامسة، أنها تحسدني على الفرصة المتاحة لي لملامسة قطع الآثار مباشرة، كان عملي وقتها يقتضي أن أتعامل مع القطع الأثرية مباشرة دون قفازات، وخارج إطارها الزجاجي، مع إجراء سلامة روتيني؛ كانت تلك الشابة المتطوعة، تنظر للقطع الأثرية بشغف وحب حقيقي، وهي تعرف قيمة ما يحدث أمامها، تعرف قيمة الأثر وعمق ملامسته مباشرة.

لم تك أيام العمل في المتحف طيلة الفترة المقررة، أياماً روتينية، الفعاليات التي أقيمت على "أساس" المشروع، لا على "هامشه" كانت حيوية وذات قيمة كبيرة، بالنسبة لي، وبالنسبة للمشروع نفسه، منها على سبيل المثال: فعالية شهدتها "The Fitzwilliam Museum" في جامعة "Cambridge"، فعالية استضافها مركز "The Mosaic Rooms" في غرب لندن، فعالية في "The Horniman Museum in south London"، لكن الفعالية التي نظمت داخل المتحف نفسه على " The Youth Factor" كان لها مذاق خاص ومختلف، كان ملهما أن يحضر الجمع منالشباب الذين ولدوا ونشأوا في المملكة المتحدة ويتعرفوا عن كثب على بعض تاريخ بلادهم العريق، أكثر من ذلك أن يعربوا عن مواهبهم في كتابة الشعر باللغتين العربية- بعض أعمالهم كانت بالعربية السودانية لا الفصحى- وبالإنجليزية، وكانت مشاركة الفنانة السودانية المعروفة "أميرة خير" وحديثها الضافي حول تجربتها وأريحيتها في الحوار مع الجمهور، حافزا لتمثُّل اللحظة واستلهامها، ضمن فعالية المشروع.

الفعاليات الأخرى، تلك التي لم تك مدرجة في البرنامج أيضاكان لها أثر فاعل، أعني فعاليات مجتمع السودانيين المهاجرين بالمملكة المتحدة، حيث شاركت عددا مقدرا من المبدعين السودانيين في

dency was the day that the inventive photographer, Crispin Hughes, came to take the photos you can now see in this book. One of the museum's volunteers who acted as an assistant, whispered to me that she was extremely envious that I was being given the opportunity to actually touch these precious objects. With great care, they were removed from the museum's glass cases and I was allowed to hold them without even wearing gloves. The assistant, who knew and clearly loved these acquisitions, fully appreciated the extraordinary experience I was given of touching them directly.

My time at the museum was far from routine. And added to this were the stimulating activities arranged at other museums, such as readings at the Fitzwilliam Museum in Cambridge, the Horniman Museum in south London and the Mosaic Rooms in west London. But probably the most exciting event was when a group of young Sudanese people called the Youth Factor came to the museum itself. It was inspiring to witness the responses of young people, born and brought up in the UK, as they encountered the ancient history of their country. More importantly, they were able to express their reactions in poetry written both in English and Arabic – and in Sudanese as well as Modern Standard Arabic. In addition, the event was graced with the participation of the Sudanese artist, Amira Kheir, who gave great insight into her experiences and warmly interacted with everyone, illuminating the project and the inspiration behind it.

One important aspect of the project was the wish to engage with the Sudanese community in the UK and, as a result, I gave many readings and shared platforms with a wide variety of Sudanese artists – poets, singers, actors and musicians. My engagement with them inspired me to complete this exciting commission.

The experience of being commissioned to write poetry was entirely new to me. Poets writing in Arabic like me expect poetry to spring entirely from personal inspiration. They do not write poetry alongside other people, let alone academics or archaeologists. At first, I felt confused and uncertain about what was expected of me. And then, as time passed, I began to master the game. Everything springs from probabilities. The world is full of surprises, is brimming with beauty and endowed with in-

مجالات مختلفة شعراً وغناء وأداء مسرحيا وغيره، في منابرهم، أثناء تواجدي بينهم، الأمر الذي أضاف لي الكثير من الحيوية، نحو أن أنجز عملي.

تجربة التفرُّغ للكتابة الشعرية تجربة جديدة بالنسبة لي، ربما بالنسبة لأبناء جيلي كذلك، نحن نشأنا أدبيا على أسس تفترض أن الكاتب يعمل دون أن يكون ملتزما بموضوع محدد سلفا، ومرتبطا بوقت محدد لإنجاز عمله الإبداعي، دون أن يكون ملتزما بفريق عمل ما، على الأخص فريق عمل أكاديمي، كأن يعمل بالقرب من علماء "الآركيولجيا"، كما حدث معي في هذه التجربة، كنت مرتبكاً لحدٍّ بعيد، حين بدأت العمل لكن رويداً، رويداً بدأت أمتلك مفاتيح اللعبة، الأمر كلّه قائم على الإحتمالات، العالم مثير للدهشة ومكتظ بالجمال ومكتنز بالإبداع؛ نعم، الذين حظيت بمقابلتهم شخصيا من الأكاديميين، وأولئك الذين راجعت كتبهم وأبحاثهم في مكتبة "المتحف" الخاصة، أو في مكتبة "مدرسة الدراسات الشرقية والإفريقية" في جامعة لندن، كانوا جميعا يلعبون على مبدأ الإحتمال "ربما" لا ينطقون عن يقين مطلق، وهو مبدأ "شعري" في اعتقادي الخاص، ألهمني الكثير من الجرأة على تقحُّم عوالمهم وابتكار عوالمي الخاصة، وأنا أدرس ما يدرسون بمنطق مختلف وزوايا موغلة في الخصوصية.

في مقابلة صحافية أجراها معي الروائي والصحافي العراقي "شاكر نوري" في مطلع الألفية الماثلة لصالح صحيفة "القدس العربي"، وكنت أعمل وقتها في إدارة القسم الثقافي لصحيفة "الأيام" العريقة في الخرطوم، الحوار وثَّق نصه موقع "جهة الشعر" الشهير لصاحبه الشاعر البحريني الكبير "قاسم حداد"، في ذلك الحوار، كتبت "أعمل على إنجاز كتاب شعري اسمه "قلادة الجعران الذهبي"" وأشرت إلى أني مهتم بإحدى ممالك السودان القديمة هي "أليس" ورد ذكرها في كتاب "الطبقات" لصاحبه محمد النور ضيف الله، تحديدا في سيرة الشيخ اسماعيل صاحب الربابة، ورد اسمها أيضا، في رواية "أخبار البنت مكايايا" للكاتب "إبراهيم إسحق" وفي كتاب"أسرار تمبكتو القديمة" للشاعر "عمر عبد الماجد".على هذه الخلفية كانت إقامتي في المتحف اضافة حقيقية لتجربتي الشعرية واضاءة معرفية لجوانب جديدة في تاريخ عريق لايكف عن إدهاش العالم بما يكتنز من أسرار.

novation. Indeed, I was fortunate to both meet academics and consult books in the Petrie's own museum and that at the School of Oriental and African Studies, who all proceeded from the principle of 'probability'. 'Maybe'. They never speak with absolute certainty at all. And, for me, this is the principle of poetry *par excellence*. As a result, I felt inspired, bolstered with the courage that enabled me to conquer their world and carve my own worlds while studying what they study – yet with another rationale, with the angels who inhabit my particular world.

At the beginning of this century when I was working at the newspaper *Al-Ayyam* in Khartoum, I was interviewed by the Iraqi novelist and journalist, Shakir Nouri for the newspaper *Al-Quds Al-Arabi*. I mentioned that I was engaged with a poetry project with the working title of 'The Golden Scarab Necklace', and I discussed my particular interest in one of Sudan's ancient kingdoms, al'Ais. My residency at the museum has allowed me to draw on these long-held interests. It has been a truly authentic and genuinely enriching addition to my experience as a poet. I have been exposed to new fields of knowledge that spring from an ancient history that will never cease surprising the world with the wealth of its secrets.

Al-Saddiq Al-Raddi in the Petrie Museum

Al-Saddiq Al-Raddi and the Sudanese Archaeological Collections at the Petrie Museum, UCL

PROFESSOR STEPHEN QUIRKE

A museum, and perhaps even a poetic tradition itself, as an institution of a kind, can grow looking inward among those who think, speak, act alike. So a poet in the museum creates a great breach in our walls of habit and complacency, in all directions. The power of that presence expands beyond measure when both the poet and the collection find themselves in another country, hostage to external forces, however generous their hosts. When I first heard Saddiq perform from heart his 'Poem of the Nile' in the Petrie Museum – to one side the objects from Meroe, on the other a painting of his verses as a map by the calligrapher Paul Antonio – from that meeting with the space of object exile, an exceptional and intensified material encounter became possible. And this encounter led Sarah Maguire of the Poetry Translation Centre and Debbie Challis of the Petrie Museum to invite Saddiq to return as Poet in Residence.

While the monuments of ancient Egypt – Kemet 'the Black Land' – dominate popular and media imagination, archaeologists have long sought to publicise the equally long and full history of Nile peoples and kingdoms upstream in Sudan. The first kings of a unified Egypt (around 3000 BC) belong to the same cultural horizon as their contemporaries in Nubia, the land either side of the modern border between Sudan and Egypt. Fifteen centuries later, based at Kerma, the rulers of Kush (northern to central Sudan) overpowered Egyptian fortresses in Nubia, threatening Thebes itself. The miraculously fine-walled, high-burnished pottery of this time, with its distinctive silvery band, continues to inspire artists such as ceramic sculptor Magdalene Odundo. Kerma was eventually conquered by New Kingdom Pharaohs, in the seesaw of war and peace between neighbours. Later kings would find inspiration in the past of both Sudan and Egypt. After 750 BC, a powerful successor to Kerma grew around the city of Napata, farther upstream, and king Piy launched a campaign to restore a divided Egypt.[1] His successors ruled both lands as the twenty-fifth Dynasty of Egyptian king-lists, until Assyrian invasion in 664 BC. The Kush kings moved their centre south to Meroe, after wars with a resurgent Egypt in the sixth century BC. The Roman Empire absorbed Egypt in 30 BC, but rulers of Meroe defeated attempts at invasion, and the kingdom continued to thrive into the third century AD. On its territory, smaller kingdoms were flourishing by the sixth century AD, when the region converted to Christianity: Alwa, centred on Soba, near Khartoum; Makuria, centred on Dongola in Upper Nubia; and Nobatia, centred on Faras in Lower Nubia. All three had weakened or dissolved by the fifteenth century AD, and a new power came to dominate all central Sudan, the Funj Sultanate of Sennar. Under Amara Dunqas, the kingdom embraced Islam in AD 1523/AH 930, and, echoing the history of Meroe against Rome, kept the Ottoman Empire at bay after Egypt fell in AD 1517/AH 922. Against the grand sweep of military history and changes in rulers, the impact on individuals and groups can only be charted in more detailed history and archaeology. At any time, Nile lands would be home to people of different customs, languages and origins, people connected overland and by river with one another and with worlds far beyond. Anchored in its archives, the museum collection offers an opportunity to encounter past people, while the poet can offer the voice of the encounter.

Of the eighty thousand objects in the Petrie Museum, some four thousand are from excavations in Sudan. Flinders Petrie (1853–1942), the first UCL professor of Egyptian archaeology, did not travel south of Aswan. However, he was fascinated by contacts between peoples, and he did encounter in Egypt the ancient imports from civilizations of Nubia. Petrie would be the first to appreciate the human story which Saddiq uncovers in the Nubian pottery and beads buried with a woman in the middle of Egypt, maybe a thousand miles from home ('Traces of an Unknown Woman' and 'The Golden Scarab Necklace'). The Petrie Museum began to receive finds from sites in Sudan only after his death, when Tony

Arkell was appointed as curator to manage the return to London of the 800 crates of objects, kept safe in English country houses during the Second World War. In Sudan, Arkell had been a colonial administrator in Darfur; later, he excavated Neolithic sites in the Khartoum area, and the National Museum of Sudan shared the finds with UCL, to promote teaching and research on Sudanese antiquity – though there is no professor of Sudan Archaeology in London. In the 1960s, the Museum received from the Wellcome Trust the Sudanese and Egyptian finds in their care; these had originally been given to the pharmaceutical magnate and collector Henry Wellcome, in return for funding excavations. The Meroe collection at the Petrie Museum is perhaps the most important part of the Wellcome transfer, comprising over six hundred objects from the 1909–1914 excavations directed by Liverpool professor John Garstang – a Petrie trainee. The largest 'item' is a set of temple wall blocks, preserving part of an image of a king wearing ceremonial collar; as the wall section is too big to reassemble on display in the present museum, the UCL website shows a reconstruction. The most striking figure is the fluteplayer, from the sculpture around a ritual pool of kingship ('They Think I Am a King: Yes I Am the King'). Some less monumental items are hard to parallel in material – as the bronze offering-table from a shrine at the city ('Schism') – or form – the game-like slab cut with spaces for seven small globes ('Killing Time') – or the combination – as the basalt vessel with its baboons ('Monkey Following a Monkey)'. Perhaps, though, we find the life of the ancient Sudanese city most keenly in works, rough or skilled, with Meroitic expressions of motifs well-known the length of the valley: a pottery offering tray that literally says 'life ('The Key of Life') or the silty stone frog ('He Tells Tales of Meroe'). Specialists on the past often speculate, and may be irritated when anyone with less factual baggage intrudes on their territory, but I think we can read here just how much we need the poet: in eight works of the word, Saddiq renews our fractured ability to see, think, and dream.

1. 'King Piy' was formerly transliterated as 'Piankhy'. See 'Poem of the Nile' p. 59.

'Stained with the Tincture of History': A Poet in the Museum[1]

SARAH MAGUIRE

In the title poem of this collection, the Sudanese poet Al-Saddiq Al-Raddi considers a beautiful frog, sculpted from fossiliferous limestone, from the fabled city of Meroe, capital of the Kingdom of Kush, who is 'now an enigmatic relic behind glass' in the Petrie Museum. The poet imagines that perhaps the frog 'tells tales of Meroe – / witness to that city's sad trajectory from glory to dejection'. That the extraordinary kingdoms that flourished in Sudan are eclipsed by their later Egyptian counterparts is made clear in the Petrie Museum's own name: it is a museum 'of Egyptian Archaeology', despite the great wealth of outstanding objects it holds from ancient Sudan – although the Petrie, to its great credit, has long put considerable effort into drawing attention to its Sudanese collections and engaging with the UK's Sudanese communities, not least in sponsoring Saddiq's residency in the museum.

Voices from Sudan are seldom heard elsewhere. News reports come in of barbaric atrocities (the Sudanese dictator, Omar al-Bashir, is currently under indictment at the International Criminal Court for crimes of genocide committed in Darfur) of corrupt, squabbling leaders who gamble with the lives of millions of people for the sake of their own petty advantage. Sudan has a long and complex history thanks to the extraordinary diversity of its people: more than two hundred languages are spoken there and the country has long been the crossing point of many major ancient trade routes both from eastern Africa to the country's western coast and from southern sub-Saharan Africa to the Mediterranean.

It is striking how the great ancient trade routes conjure violence. Their very strategic significance is their value and Afghanistan, like Sudan (and now Syria) have been plagued by their geographical position. In his poem, 'Children in Exile', James Fenton writes of 'Those whom geography condemns to war' and it is the rich diversity of Sudan's cultures that spring from the peoples who have crossed its land, that provokes retribution from those who wish to control such valuable territory.

The Nubian grave goods held in the Petrie's collections that were discovered many miles from their resting place in Middle Egypt, fascinated the poet and, from them, emerged one of the most powerful poems in this collection, 'Traces of an Unknown Woman'. In this poem, Saddiq imagines the 'richly attired' woman who once owned these precious objects setting out on the Darb al Arbain ('Road of Forty Days'). The poem refers to 'An epoch of atrocities witnessed by the diggers of graves' and then lists atrocities that are horribly familiar from today's news: 'temples razed to the ground', 'violated women' – carried out by those whose creed is 'the discourse of separation and selection' for whom difference is 'decreed by the naked eye'.

The fantasies of 'purity' that are the bedrock of fascist thinking are inimical to difference and in this, al-Bashir is no exception. His rule has been marked by a determination to turn Sudan into a monotheist, monocultural Islamicist society with Arabic the country's one accepted language and Arabism its objective. Shortly after he came to power in 1989, he banned the Writers' Union, shut down libraries and had all the books they housed destroyed, other than textbooks on maths, Arabic and Islam.

Al-Saddiq Al-Raddi is widely regarded as one of the most important African poets writing in Arabic. And although the Arabic of his poetry is stringently classical, he writes from the position of being an African. He has an inexhaustible knowledge of the peoples and languages of his vast country and, unlike most Sudanese, has travelled the length and breadth of what once was northern Sudan (South Sudan seceded in 2011). He is steeped in Sudanese music and art and alive to the cultures of nearby countries, such as Mali and Mauritania, which are inextricably connected with his own.

By the time I founded the Poetry Translation Centre in 2004, I had nearly a decade's experience of co-translating Arabic, mainly Palestinian, poetry. Thanks to my friendship with Crispin Hughes, whose stunning photographs illustrate this book, I'd also developed an interest in Sudan (Crispin had visited southern Sudan – then still at war with the north –

on behalf of Oxfam and other charities, many times since the 1990s). Given my interests, I was eager for the PTC to translate a poet writing in Arabic from Sudan, particularly because so little Sudanese poetry had ever been translated into English. I was delighted when Hafiz Kheir, who'd been attending the poetry translation workshops I'd set up at SOAS in 2002, introduced us to the astonishing poetry of Al-Saddiq Al-Raddi. I commissioned Hafiz to co-translate Saddiq with Mark Ford and we invited him to the UK to take part in the PTC's first World Poets' Tour in 2005. Saddiq's beautiful poetry gained him a wide audience among non-Arabic speakers; but, perhaps more significantly, his arrival here was greeted with huge enthusiasm by the UK Sudanese community, who were familiar with his poetry and with his principled opposition to al-Bashir's dictatorship.

In the poet's introduction to this volume, he mentions how his most famous work 'Poem of the Nile' – written around the time of al-Bashir's coup – was the origin of his relationship with the Petrie Museum. Beautifully translated by Mark Ford and Hafiz Kheir, the poem is a lament for Khartoum, a city that has sunk into 'the ruins of a beautiful, vanished past'. In the poem, Saddiq remembers the kingdom of Kush, its capital Meroe and King Piankhy, who ruled over Egypt. In other words, to the poet, Sudan today is inseparable from its complex – often magnificent, often violent – history. Steeped as he is in this history, no one could have been a better choice to act as the Petrie Museum's poet in residence – the results of which you now hold in your hands.

---

1. From 'A Monkey Following a Monkey'.

Al-Saddiq Al-Raddi with the figure of a flute player from Meroe.

Al-Saddiq Al-Raddi examines Nubian grave goods found in Middle Egypt.

مفتاح الحياة

لابُدَّ مِنْ نَهرٍ لتنضجَ
لابدَّ مِنْ تميمةٍ ليسطعَ جوهرُها
لتكتملَ الأحجية!
الإلهُ- المَلِكُ أم المَلِكُ- الإلهْ؟!
أيهما السَّابقُ..
أيهما بيدِهِ مقبضَ البابِ
أو شفرة الأبديَّةْ؟!

... ...

السَّابِقُ مازال لغزاً
كان تميمةً
مرآةً معدنيةً
مُذَّهباً أو مصقولاً بالنُّحاسِ
أيقونةَ شمسٍ بمدافنَ أَعْرَقُ
السَّابقُ مجرى نَهْرٍ سَابِقْ!

The Key of Life

Civilisation springs from a river:
the brilliant glint of an amulet
permits this story to be told
Who came first – a God or a King?
Who opens the door?
Who holds the key to the mystery of eternity?

. . .   . . .

The firstborn is an enigma
        an amulet
                a mirror
        fused from burnished copper
        an icon of the sun buried in a grave
a grave in a riverbed in the grave of a river

The Key of Life
Pottery offering tray, with internal walls in a Meroitic form of the ancient Egyptian hieroglyph for the word 'ankh' (life). The upper surface bears traces of red paint. 500 BC–AD 100. UC43990

Traces of an Unknown Woman
Two Nubian pottery vessels, and a string of beads placed in the isolated burial of a woman near village cemeteries north of Qau, in Middle Egypt: highly polished black silt scoop, of a form known from central Sudan UC17888; black-topped bowl with hole punched through wall, perhaps to avoid recycling by the living UC17889; beads UC26013 (and see 'The Golden Scarab Necklace') 1800-1600 BC

أثرُ امرأةٍ غريبة

1

الحارسُ يتعلَّقُ بـ الفانوسْ
الفارسُ بعنُقِ الجَوادْ
نُوديتُ بـ الأُمِّ من كهفِ نَسْلٍ بعيدٍ
مِنْ حداءِ القوافلِ أو خوفِها
مِنْ صمتِها بَرقَ الجُعْرانُ الذهبيّ

العشيرةُ زادٌ وقِلادةْ
المَسيرةُ وشمٌ
ودأبُ نجاةٍ على سِنِّ رُمْحٍ!

2

كلُّ ألفيةٍ، ثمة أنثى تَعْبُرُ "دَرْبَ الأربعينْ"
مُحَفَّلَةً في الغدوِّ أو الرواحِ
وقد لا تعودْ
كلُّ ألفيةٍ تَنْسَخُ أُخرى

... ...

ما تبقَّى: مَعْرِفَةٌ لم تَبُحْ بَعْدُ بأسرارِها
إناءٌ فخَّاريٌّ - نَقبُهُ مِنْ أثرِ ألفيةٍ عَبَرَتْ وتزيدُ
قلادةٌ منظومةٌ مِنْ صَدَفِ النَّهرِ ومِنْ بحارٍ بعيدةٍ - فخارٌ ملوَّنٌ بأكسيدِ النّحاسِ - قِشرُ بيضِ النَّعَامِ،.. إلخ.
ما تبقَّى يَشِفُّ ويكشفُ!

Traces of an Unknown Woman

1

The watchman cleaves to his lantern
The knight clings to the neck of his horse
My name was passed down from mother to daughter –
like the songs sung by caravans to bolster their courage
My name is the gleam of a golden scarab

The tribe is both sustenance and a finely-wrought necklace
The journey is like a tattoo
Survival is balanced on the point of a spear

2

Each millennium a woman journeyed along Darb Al Arbain[1]
Richly attired as she travelled the road back and forth
She may not return
Each millennium she starts out once more

… … …

What remains: a ladle that keeps its own counsel
A clay pot punctured by millennia
A necklace of shells from distant seas, of shells gleaned from a far-off riverbed – pottery stained with the patina of copper – the blown egg of an ostrich, etc, etc
What remains: revelation

3

رأسُ الحكمةِ
مزَّقه رأسُ الخنجرْ..
... ...

.. **في ذلك العصرْ** جَرَتْ وقائعَ كثيرةٌ كما رأى حفّارو مقابرْ. حُطِّمتْ معابدَ. حكى رجالٌ بأصابعَ يتطايرُ منها الشجرُ المحترقْ. نسوةٌ أيضاً شُوهدتْ أسرارهنّ لولا ضيقَ ذات اليدْ. جاء خُطّابُ العناصرِ جاءَ خطّاؤونَ كراريسُهم رُكِّبتْ جُمْلَةً على ناقةِ المَفْسَدَة. جرى تفحُّصُ السلالاتِ بالعينِ المجرَّدة- مُرِّغتْ أُنوفُها. ألسنةٌ لا تُحصَى جُعلتْ تحت حوافرِ الخيل. بطونٌ نُسبتْ لبطونْ.

3

The fount of wisdom is pierced by
the point a dagger

... ...

An epoch of atrocities witnessed by the diggers of graves. Temples razed to the ground. Tales told by men whose fingers fire flames. Violated women branded by poverty, scorned with shame. Then came the discourse of separation and selection. Then came camp followers, wielding division, corrupt catalogues of sins straddled on camels, difference decreed by the naked eye. Numberless tongues were ripped out to be trammelled under the hooves of horses.

The end of a tribe is a tribe.

1. This group of Nubian pottery and beads is from a burial of a woman, recorded by archaeologist Guy Brunton as no.1989 in his publication of cemeteries on the east bank of the Nile between Qau and Asyut in Middle Egypt. Here, desert roads connect the river valley, west to the oases, east towards the Red Sea, and on both sides onward south to Sudan; the most famous of these routes is Darb al Arbain 'Road of Forty Days', leading from Darfur in western Sudan to the Kharga Oasis and across to Asyut. No other Nubian burial is recorded in this or the nearest cemeteries, but the desert foothills in the area sheltered some small, perhaps seasonal settlements of desert Nubians. The other grave goods were leather sandals (Egyptian burials of this date avoid animal skins), a bone awl, two Spatha shells from the Red Sea, and a north Egyptian scarab. The body of the woman was not recorded in detail, so her precise age and ethnicity are unknown, but those who buried her were following desert Nubian customs.

يظنونني ملكاً وأنا الملك

حاجتي للكلمةِ
حاجةُ السَّابقِ للحَجَرِ والنَّارِ
حاجتُه للبَلْطةِ والرُّمْحِ والدرعِ
للأُنْسِ بالنايِّ..

أَثريتُكِ
أَثريتُ ظنَّ الحياةِ بأيّامِها والذئب بلياليه
أَثريتُ جوعَ الفرادةِ
بقيتُ لا للموعظةِ أو ثمن الفراءِ
بقيتُ فأبقيتُ كَسْبَ السبيَّة حَيّاً
..
ما أكلتهُ الحروبُ بقاياكَ
ما ألهمَ المُهْمَلَ
واحدٌ من رعايا فتنتكِ المُفترِسَة!
فطنتني
أخذتني بعيداً بجهلي
يظنونني ملكاً وأنا المَلِكُ.

They Think I Am a King: Yes, I Am the King

I need the Word
like my ancestor's need for stone and fire
like his need for an axe, for a spear, for a shield
like his need for the solace of a flute...

I enriched you
like life is enriched by day
like a wolf is enriched by a night with no moon
I enriched the longing for transcendence
I stayed neither to preach nor to barter with the skins of animals
I stayed to bear witness to the dignity of women enslaved

..

Wars consumed your remains
Their traces captivated your disciples
in thrall to your fierce charm
You taught me
You delivered me from ignorance
They think I am a king:
Yes, I am the King

They think I Am a King: Yes, I Am the King
Painted sandstone figure of a flute-player, from the royal ritual bath at Meroe. The head was stolen from the museum in the 1960s.
100 BC–AD 100. UC8964

He Tells Tales of Meroe
Figure of crouching frog, in a hard fossiliferous limestone. Perhaps an image to ensure the fertility of the rains and the Nile flood.
500 BC–AD 100. UC43984

كأنَّما يروي عن مروي

كأنَّما صوت نقيقه يطلعُ من كسوتِه الحجريةْ
كأنَّما طبقات صوتِه تتلوَّنُ في الظلمةِ مغسولةً في طبقاتِ الأبديةْ

حينما رأيتُه ساهماً ووحيداً
في "فترينة" المتحفِ
تذكرتُ نطفتَه الأولى مختلطةً بطينتِه الأمِّ
كان يقنصُ الفرائسَ باللُّعابِ
يموِّهُ مفترسيه باللَّون وأحابيلَ أخرى
يستيقظُ مثل أقرانه مِنْ سُباته الموسميّ
لموسم التزاوج الجديدْ
قبل أن يصبح أثراً غامضاً خلف الزجاجْ

كأنَّما يروي عن مروي
شاهداً على غروبها مرةً ومرة على شموخِ مجدها..
كأنَّه في سُباته الأخيرِ يتأهبُ ثانيةً
للحياة بلباسٍ وتاجٍ جديدْ- بلسانٍ جديدْ.

He Tells Tales of Meroe

As if his croak sounds from stone itself
As if his voice in darkness is stained with the timbre of eternity

When I first saw him alone, lost in thought,
poised behind glass,
I recalled how his sperm had once spawned from the suck of motherly mud
to snatch prey with spit
A camouflaged trickster,
awakening each spring with his mates
to a spring of mating

Now an enigmatic relic behind glass,
perhaps he tells tales of Meroe –
witness to that city's sad trajectory from glory to dejection

In this, his last siesta,
he readies himself for life
with his new cloak, a new tongue and his crown

شَرْخ

جدُّكَ يَحْلِبُ أَبْقَارَهُ مُنْتَصِباً

يَجْرِدُ الزَرْعَ و الضَرْعْ

أسلافُهُ مَبْدَأُ الصّنْعَةِ

أَخْيَارُ حَقْلَ ابنُ آدم

بما خَبروا من قُوَّةِ الصَّقر – حِكمة الغُرَابْ

أتلك مائدة القرابين؟!

... ...

جدّتُكَ الغابرةْ

كانت تُعِدُّ لها القرمصيص – عِزِّ أمّها

إرْثُ عِزَّتَها – صبوَتها العاشقةْ

تُعِدُّ لها قطرةَ الدَم

جذْرُ خصوبَتِها البِكْر لا البَكَارَة؛

تَحْثو ضَارِعَةً لتُبَارَكْ؛ لِيُبَارَكَ خَيْطُ السُّلالةِ!

أتلك سجَّادة جدُّتكَ الحَاضِرَةُ؟!

Schism[2]

Your grandfather
strode erect as he drove his cattle
numbering his herds and his grain
His ancestors, master craftsmen,
the pride of Adam's farm
strong as eagles
as wise as the raven
... ...
Your grandmother
prepared the *garmasis* – the bridal garment
precious heirloom of your mother
witness to her desire and your integrity –
that itself awaited
the drop of virgin blood
as she knelt
blessed with humility
blessing her bloodline

Is this his sacrificial altar?
Or the prayer mat of your grandmother?

---

2. The title 'Schism' points to the fissures over the brittle deep green surface of the object. It was prompted here in particular by the crack across the outward offering-channel above the depiction of the offering-table, alerting us to the fragility of the archaeological find.

Schism

Bronze offering table, bearing a depiction of the offering table, flowers and water-jars used for making libations and offerings to deities and the deceased. Found at a river sanctuary at Meroe, in excavations directed by John Garstang 1913–1914 (his 'Shrine 1000'). 200 BC–AD 100. UC43987

Killing Time

Sandstone slab with six hemispheres cut around a seventh, perhaps for a board-game and/ or rituals of divination. 500 BC–AD100. UC44305
Six quartz and chert balls of different colours: these fit the cups in the slab, but were not found with it. 500 BC–AD100. UC44306

قيلولة الآلهة

ثَمَّةَ الحَجَرُ المَلِكْ
المَلِكةُ الحَصاةْ

قادةُ الجُنْدِ يفعلون الحرب
صُكَّتْ النّقودُ - وقتها - حُلْيَةً
لِجِرارِ وَقْتٍ مُمِلِ
وقتٌ أظمأُ للدَمِ
تَنْقدُهُ رؤوسَ متطايرةً: مَلِكاً
إثْرَ مَلِكْ
وقتٌ تنقدُهُ سبيكةَ الوقتْ

لتكتملَ اللعبةَ: لابُدَّ من حُفْرةٍ خاليةْ
لابُدَّ مِنْ حَصاةٍ وحَجَرْ
لابُدَّ مِنْ أضحيةٍ وقربانْ
نصيبُكَ حفرةٌ خاليةْ
مَهْرُكِ سِرٌّ كشفتهُ الكنايةْ

أخيراً؛ ثمة حجرٍ يحنُّ إلى كهفه
ثَمَّ حَصاةٍ تحنُّ إلى شاطيء النَّهرِ
أخيراً جَرَّةٌ مُفْتقدةٌ - مطمورةُ السِرِّ ؟!
ليست تلك هي المعضلة:
ثمة ملكٍ معطوبٍ ثمة تاجٍ يُتَوَّجُ للهاويَّة!

Killing Time

Here a stone is King,
the Queen, a pebble

When there's time to kill,
coins become trinkets
hoarded in vases
and commanders make war
Killing time
by scattering the heads
of one king after the next
they fall for ingots of time

When the final hole is taken
by stone or pebble –
by a sacrifice or an offering –
then the game is up
Your lot
is that vacant hole
Your dowry,
the mystery of a metaphor

In the end there is a stone, aching for its cave
a pebble, longing for the riverbank
In the end, an abandoned earthenware pot
repository of enigmas
But that's just a game –
reality is a crippled king
and a crown that straddles the abyss

قردٌ إثرَ قردٍ

الإضاءةُ وحدها/ الظلُّ وحده
لا تسألي عن بَصْمَةِ الجِسْمِ
لا عن أثرَ اللّسانْ!

...

مُهْرةٌ تُرَوَّضُ
لا أقلّ من مِلكةٍ تُتوَّجُ
وتسألني حَبّةُ قمحٍ أسفلَ كرسيِّ العَرْشْ
أسألُ سيّدةَ الصولجانْ!

...

ليس نَقْشاً يَدلُّ لا أثرَ يُقْتَنى
قُدْرَةُ تقطيرِ حَدْسِ النَجَاةْ
بيدي ألمسُ: لم نكُ عابرين أو عبثاً
أصغي لمزمورة النَبْضِ
أحدسُ أمثولة الأبديَة!

A Monkey Following a Monkey

A solitary light / a shadow in solitude
do not ask for an imprint on the body
do not ask for a trace of the tongue

...
Taming a stallion
is nothing less than crowning the Queen
You demand that grain of wheat found under the throne –
I demand she who bears the mace

...
No inscription to denote, no relic to possess
only the ability to distil the hunch of survival
We were not passers-by – we did not live in vain:
With this hand I touch,
listening to the psalm of pulsation
intuiting the lesson of eternity

...

آنيةُ السِّرِّ محفوفةً بالزغاريدِ والتعاويذْ

إناءُ النبيذْ

يحفُّ نفسه بإجلالْ

على السقفِ ألسنةُ نارِ الشموعِ الخفيضةِ

تُلهبُ صدرَ العاشِقِ

يسرقُ جذْرَ الخصوبةِ

بأغنيةٍ على وشكِ الإندثارْ!

... ...

النَّهرُ لم يمتزجْ بالنَّهرِ

منذ صُنْعِ المراكبِ، صَيدِ وطبخِ السَّمكْ

مؤونةُ العامِ مِنْ خيراتِ المواسمِ والفاكهةْ

خِبْرَة حَفْرِ الخنادقْ

النَّهرُ دَمٌ يعقبهُ نَدَمُ التاريخِ

أرضٌ يرثها الثَّأرُ

وامرأةٌ تلوبُ مغلوبةً تزأرُ في كهفِها

هل كنتُ حاضراً هناك؟!

…
The secret vessels are riddled with cries and spells
The wine urn
shrouds itself in solemnity
The candles' tongues gutter on the ceiling
inflaming the heart of the suitor
who highjacks the root of fertility with a song on the verge of extinction

… … …
This river never mingled with the river
Ever since boats were invented, fishing and the preparation of fish,
and the fruitful bounty of plenty was harvested,
since channels were cut and dredged
this river is Blood, stained with the tincture of history
a land inherited by vengeance
a woman helplessly roaming and roaring in a cave

Was I there – there and then?

A Monkey Following a Monkey
Basalt tapering cylinder vessel, the exterior sculpted in high relief with images of a male baboon on hind legs, holding forward a vessel of the same form. The scene may be a Meroitic version of the main ancient Egyptian myth of healing, in which Thoth in baboon form brings the eye of the sun-god back from Nubia, as the fertile Nile flood returns each summer from south to north. 500 BC–AD 100. UC44307

The Golden Scarab Necklace
Blue and black faience and red carnelian beads, with shells pierced for stringing. The materials are typical of both Sudanese and Egyptian production, but the treatment, range and forms are typical especially for nomadic groups in the eastern Nubian desert. Placed with two Nubian pottery vessels in the burial of a woman, north of Qau in Middle Egypt (see 'Traces of an Unknown Woman'). 1800–1600 BC.
UC26013

قلادة الجُعْران الذهبيِّ

1

أغادرُ..
مِنْ لغةٍ تعرفُني لـ اللّغة الأمِّ
أمُّنا لم تَعُدْ واحدةْ!
... ...
أتعلَّم صمت خنجرك الوغد
لن تعرف وجهي
كنت تعرف صوتي حين كنت أخيكْ
تركة الأبِّ لن تشفع لي أو لك
يشفع أثر الغراب!

... ...
أغادرُ..
مؤتزراً بطلسم اللغة المروية
بصفو جريان النَّهر
وثيقة النَّهرِ الحقِّ – بيننا
بيننا دَمٌ
متحفُ الجمجمة الأمِّ
بيننا إفك العروشْ!

2

كردفالُ سيِّدةُ المعبدِ أو ربما مروي
البخورُ تجودُ به فازوغلي
أليسُ تحرسُ مائدةَ القرابينِ مزهوةً
الطينُ يسطعُ- فَخَّارُه يسطع مفتخراً بدمِكَ النبويِّ.

The Golden Scarab Necklace

1

I return
from a language that knows me,
the mother tongue,
although our mother is no longer the same
… .… …
I am learning the silence of your vulgar dagger
You will never recognise my face
even though you knew me by the sound of my voice when I was your brother
Our father's inheritance is no longer enough to mediate between us
Now, nothing is left save the trace of a raven
..… .….
I take my leave
cloaked in the enigma of the language of Meroe,
with the force and clarity of a river in spate
Bad blood lies between us –
The strife and lies of corruption

2

Like Meroe, Kurdofal[3] has many temples
Fazoghli grants incense
Al'Ais proudly guards the sacrificial feast
Stone glows
Pottery shines with the proud blood of prophecy

... ...
وَلَدٌ أنجبَ السلطنةْ
بدم أنجبته السلطنات العريقة
مؤتزراً بجلال رايات أسلافه
ولدٌ أنجب السلطنات العريقة والمستحيلة والممكنة!

3

المَلِكُ في حمّامه الصباحيِّ مستغرقٌ في المُلْكْ
مرآةٌ على حائطِ المعجزةْ
تسلبُ عذراءَ عطرَ الصباباتِ
... ...
لثوري أخضِّبُ شَعرَي، سبيكةً لا سبيَّة
سريره أضرّجه بالخُمْرَة والدُّخانْ
جرارُ الغَنَج مُعَدَّةٌ
قرونُه سليلةُ العَنَجِ ورفْسُهُ ابنُ شمسِ الإستواءْ
... ...
هذه ليلتكَ
رأسُ المَلِكِ المدلَّلِ كأسي
وأنا جُعْرانةُ المملكةْ!

3. Now a monumental archaeological site, the ancient city of Meroe, near Begrawiya in central Sudan, was the centre of the vast kingdom that ruled central and northern Sudan about 300 BC to AD 200. Kordofan is one area of that realm, in central Sudan, poised in more recent centuries between the Funj Sultans of Sennar to the east, and the Sultans of Darfur to the west. In the Sennar Sultanate, Fazoghli formed the southern border region on the Upper Blue Nile towards Ethiopia and the sources of incense. Al'Ais evokes al 'Ais, on the White Nile at the western approach to Jebel Moya, a site to the southwest of Sennar, excavated for Henry Wellcome. Jebel Moya finds in the Petrie Museum include the jewellery buried with an elder woman, from the first millennium BC. As well as the Nile, overland routes such as the Darb al-Arbain (see Traces of an Unknown Woman) linked these southern

... ...
The boy fathered a sultanate
from the bloodline that fathered ancient sultanates
The glory of his ancestral banners
is that boy who fathered the ancient sultanates: kingdoms both impossible
and possible

3

The king in his pomp wallows in his bath
A mirror glints on the wall of miracles
reflecting a virgin, her perfumed lust, her desire
... ...
To please my stud I dyed my hair with gold
I anointed his bed with incense and sandalwood
... ...
This is his night:
I take the scull of my pampered king
for my goblet –
for I am the golden scarab of this kingdom!

lands to the Saharan oases and Egypt. These desert roads encouraged seasonal migration and trade connections between distant peoples, immortalised in the burial of a woman with Nubian pottery and beads at the mouth of a desert valley north of Qau in Middle Egypt.

The scarab or dung beetle is an ancient Egyptian symbol of solar kingship, used from about 2000 BC as the form for stone seals, which were also worn as protective talismans. Already by 1700 BC the kingdom of Kerma in northern Sudan was producing its own versions of these seals. A thousand years later, the palace artists of Napatan kings created new designs in both Egypt and Sudan, where young women were particularly often protected as if sealed by a sacred scarab - as in the Qau burial.

Al-Saddiq Al-Raddi holds punctured Nubian pot found in Middle Egypt.

Al-Saddiq Al-Raddi with basalt vessel from Meroe.

قصيدة النيل

سورة:

تصعدُ الجدرانُ في اللبلاب
والخرطوم واقفةٌ
على ساقٍ تغنِّي
هل ينامُ النيلُ؟!
كُنَّا عاشقَيْنِ نهدهدُ الأطفالَ
- ما اسْمي؟!
- أُسمِّيكِ حضورَ الأرضِ فاقتربي
- وما طعمُ البكاءِ؟!
- ... ...
إفترقنا!.

سورة:

النيلُ يمضي هادئاً
ينسابُ في صمتِ المدينة
واحتراقاتِ القرى
والأصدقاءُ الآن
لا يتبادلونَ تحيةَ الصُّبْحِ
ولا يتعارفونَ
وأنبياءُ الفَقْرِ في كُلِّ الأماكنِ
يرشفون الشَّايَ والحزنَ
ولا يتحدَّثونَ
يخبِّئونَ الموتَ في أطرافِهم
ويوزِّعونَ الصَّبْرَ للأطفالِ
ينتشرونَ في الأشجارِ عَبْرَ الأرضِ

Poem of the Nile

Prelude:

Walls climb the ivy
And Khartoum, poised on its unamputated foot
        Singing
Will the Nile ever escape into sleep?
We were the most loving of lovers, children trickling from us
        –   What name do you give me?
        –   I call you Presence of Earth
        –   Come closer then
        –   What will be the taste of grief?
        –   ....
And we parted!

Sura:

The Nile flows quietly
    Seeping through the city's silence
        And the burning sorrows of villages.

Now friends no longer exchange greetings each morning
    No longer recognise each other.
        Everywhere one sees them, these one-time prophets,

Poverty-stricken, sipping their tea, their tears,
    Speechless.
        They hide death in their fraying clothes,

And all they can say to our children is: patience.
    They fade into the trees, commit suicide
        At night, derive from alcohol

Their arguments, embark on futile wars
    With their women, give up
        Their prayers, then disappear.

ينتحرونَ في اللَّيْلِ احتجاجاً
ثُمَّ يَنْتَحِلونَ عَقْلَ زَجاجةِ الخَمْرِ،
ويفتعلونَ حَرْباً في النساءِ،
ولا يقيمونَ الصَّلاةَ
ويرحلونْ.

تصعدُ الجدرانُ في اللبلابِ
والخرطومُ جالسةٌ على مقهىً تدخِّنُ
إستوى في اللَّيلِ قُطَّاعُ الطَّريقِ
وعابرو نصفَ المسافةِ
هل يكونُ الشارعُ الآن امتداداً
لاختناقِ اللَّيلِ بالعرباتِ والعُهرِ
وكنَّا عاشقَيْنِ، نفتِّش الأطفالَ
والأطفالُ في رئةِ المخابزِ

يسرقونَ النَّارَ
- ما اسْمي؟!
- أُسمِّيكِ احتراقَ الأرضِ، فانتفضي
- وما طعمُ الرَّمادِ؟!
- ... ...
إفترقنا!.

سورة:

الماءُ ضدَّ النَّارِ
والأمواجُ خارطةٌ تفرُّ من البلادْ
النَّارُ ضدَّ الماءِ
والدخان ذاكرةٌ تؤسِّسُ للرماد
الصَبيَّةُ بين سِكِّيني وقلبي

Walls climb the ivy
And Khartoum, sitting in a café
          Smoking
In the dark you can't tell apart
Muggers from those whose journeys they'd cut short.
We were lovers, looking for our children
Who were breaking into bakeries, stealing fire
From the ovens' throats.
              – What name do you give me?
              – I call you earth's Fiery Anger
              – So rise up
              – What will be the taste of ashes?
              – ……………………
                    And we parted!

Sura:

Fire is the opposite of Water
And Smoke is a memory that prepares us only for ash.
Water is the opposite of Fire
And the waves are like maps, rippling across the land.
And the girl? She is somewhere between this heart and this knife. . .

City – you're a handful of grains of wheat, tucked
    Into the purses of usurers and slave-traders.
        And the black men

Are approaching, approaching. River Nile
    To what deserts are you taking my reflections? You depart
        And I stand among the horses, by your gate,

And my soul would embark on a holy journey too,
    For the silence suspended between us
        Is a language floating among the ruins of a beautiful, vanished past.

والمدينةُ قبضةُ القمحِ
بحافظةِ المرابينَ وتجّارِ العبيدْ
والرِّجالُ السُّمْرُ يقتربون يقتربون
يا نيلُ ..
إلى أيِّ الصّحارى
تحملُ الآن تصاويري وتمضي
وقفتي بين الجيادِ أمامَ بابِكَ
عُمْرَةٌ للرُّوحِ
والصَّمْتُ المعلَّقُ بيننا
لغةٌ من الزمنِ الجميلِ إلى الزمان المستحيلْ

يا أيها النيلُ – أبي
هل كانت الأشجارُ نافذةً
لأحزانِ النساءِ
أم المرايا هشَّمت في الماءِ
تاريخَ الحضورِ الأنثويِّ
وتَثبَّتَتْ في العشبِ لونَ الفقر
إنَّ الفقرَ ينبُتُ في أراجيحِ الصِّغارِ
يورِّثُ الأطفالَ
صمتَ اللعنةِ الكبرى وكُفْرَ الأوَّلينْ.

سورة:

النيلُ يفتح ساعديه
يحدِّثُ الطَّيرَ المهاجرَ
ثم يصمتُ
يعتلي عرشَ المكانِ
ولا ينامُ ..ولا ينامْ
النيل يَسكَرُ بالنفاياتِ

O River Nile, father
Were the trees merely windows reflecting women's sorrows,
Or have your waters shattered their images,
Drowned the history of women,
And painted forever their meadows the colour of poverty?
Poverty invades the children's playgrounds, leaving
Them silent, accursed, their heritage
Only anger and disbelief.

Sura:

The Nile opens his arms
Speaks to the migrant birds
              Falls silent
Reigns
      And never sleeps
      Never sleeps

The Nile drinks dry the desert's tavern,
Gets drunk on dumps of toxic waste,
Must survive in the city, falling apart
Each night, rising up through its history
      And never sleeps
      Never sleeps

The drums began with the sun
And its light filtered songs that entered into the pores of the soul.
In the river's shallows boats sheltered from toil and wind.
Now the carnivals of the blacks take fire
And the Nile has burst through the layers of time.

ويَقْنَعُ بالمدينةِ وانكسارِ اللَّيلِ
يصعدُ في الزَّمانِ
ولا ينامُ ..ولا ينامْ
طلعتْ من الشمس الطُّبُولُ
ورقرقَ الضوءُ الغناءَ على مَسَامِ الرُّوحٍ
والماءُ استراحاتُ المراكبِ من عناءِ الرِّيحِ
فجَّرَ النيلُ الزمانَ
وقد أطلَّتْ - فجأةً - مَرَوِي
ووجه العاشقِ النوبيِّ
إذْ يمشي على حزنِ السواقي
وهو يبحثُ في الجيادِ عن الرجولةِ
أين تبدأُ دورةُ الدَّمِ يا بعانخي
أين يحتدمُ النزيفُ
وأنت مستندٌ على "كُوْشَ"
التي اهترأتْ من الصمتِ المريرِ

قل للجياد تحرَّكي ،
تَقِفُ المياهُ على أناملِها
وتنشطرُ الخرائطُ هل تضيعُ الأرضُ،
والنيلُ اكتمالٌ للقرون القادمةُ؟!
النيلُ يعرفُ سوءةَ المدنِ التي ضاعتْ
ويعرفُ موقفَ الزَّمنِ القَديمِ
ولا يحدِّثُ
إنه النيلُ
وللأجيالِ أن تمضي
وللأطفالِ أن يقفوا على الشَّطِّ طويلاً في انتظارِ العاقبة!

And, see, the kingdom of Meroe appears
And the face of the Nubian lover
Who walks among the sorrows of the waterwheels
Searching for warriors among the horses.
Where does the line of ancestral blood begin
And when does the blood loss reach its climax,
O King Piankhy, enthroned ruler of Kush,
A kingdom unravelling in bitter silence?

Shout at the horses, and let
The waters ready themselves.
Let the maps explode. How can the land be lost
When the future belongs to the Nile?

The Nile knows of the disgrace of cities
That have vanished.
Knows of the old times
Yet never speaks.
It is the Nile. . .
Generations will pass, and there will always be children
Lingering on its banks,
Waiting
For it all to end.

Meroe: Capital city of the ancient Sudanese Kingdom of Kush.
King Piankhy: Kushite king who conquered Egypt; his name is now commonly transliterated as 'Piy' (see p. 14).

Al-Saddiq Al-Raddi in the Petrie Museum.

Acknowledgements

Professor Stephen Quirke, Research Curator of the Petrie Museum, first contacted the Poetry Translation Centre in 2005 when he discovered we were inviting a poet from Sudan to take part in our first World Poets' Tour – so we have Stephen to thank for inaugurating the very fruitful relationship that's developed between our two organisations over the past decade.

We are enormously grateful to Stephen for allowing Saddiq – and our photographer, Crispin Hughes – access to the very fragile and precious objects in the Petrie's Sudanese collections, and for his warmth, support and encouragement throughout. Debbie Challis, the Petrie's indefatigable Public Programmer, put together the successful grant application to the Arts Council. Debbie has been a constant source of inventive ways of increasing the project's audience in partnership with Visitor Service Officer Tanya Golding, who worked closely with Saddiq during his residency in 2012, welcoming visitors and workshop participants alike. Salma Daoud liaised with the UK Sudanese community during Saddiq's residency, arranging special events and drawing in new audiences across the country. We'd also like to thank Eyman Osman for arranging such a stimulating workshop at the Petrie with the British Sudanese community group the Youth Factor.

Many thanks to Arts Council England for their generous support of this project.

Biographies

AL-SADDIQ AL-RADDI is widely regarded as one of the leading African poets writing in Arabic. Famous since a teenager, he is admired for the lyric intensity of his poetry and for his principled opposition to Sudan's dictatorship. His *Collected Poems* was published in Arabic in 2010. A distinguished journalist, he was forced into exile in 2012 and now lives in London.

STEPHEN QUIRKE is Edwards Professor of Egyptian Archaeology and Philology at UCL. From 1989–1999 he was curator for hieratic manuscripts at the British Museum, and in 1999–2012 he was curator for the digitisation and planned move of the Petrie Museum collections. His current research is in Middle Kingdom social history, and the history of archaeology in the Nile Valley, with a focus on the ancient and modern workforce.

SARAH MAGUIRE is the founder and director of the Poetry Translation Centre and editor of the anthology *My Voice: A Decade of Poems from the Poetry Translation Centre* (Bloodaxe Books, 2014). Author of four highly praised poetry collections, her selected poems, *Almost the Equinox*, was published by Chatto & Windus in 2015.

MARK FORD has published three collections of poetry, *Landlocked* (1992), *Soft Sift* (2001), and *Six Children* (2011). He has also written a biography of the French poet, playwright and novelist, Raymond Roussel, and translated Roussel's *New Impressions of Africa*. He teaches in the English Department at University College London.

RASHID EL SHEIKH migrated from Sudan to the UK in 1991 as a political refugee. He obtained a diploma in International Studies from Birkbeck College and an MA in Cultural Policy Management from City University. He is Senior Coordinator of the International Relations Department at the Wellington Hospital in London.

ATEF ALSHAER is a Lecturer in Arabic Language and Culture at the University of Westminster. His many publications include the forthcoming books *Poetry and Politics in the Modern Arab World* and *Language and National Identity in Palestine: Representations of Power and Resistance in Gaza*. He was ducated at Birzeit University in Palestine and at SOAS where he obtained his PhD and taught for a number of years.

HAFIZ KHEIR was born in 1968 in Khartoum and moved to the UK in 1992. A translator and filmmaker, he graduated from the Film & Television School at the London Institute in 2000. He studied drama and theatre from 1982 to 1986 at the Youth Palace, Omdurman.

CRISPIN HUGHES has worked extensively in sub-Saharan Africa producing photographs for a wide range of charities, including Oxfam and the World Food Programme. In the UK his work has focussed on social issues, such as homelessness, housing and health, for clients including the Fire Brigade, Help the Aged and the Royal Free Hospital. Co-founder of Photofusion in Brixton, he is a mentor for the New Londoners project which encourages refugees to use photography to document their experiences. His work appears regularly in the national and international press.

This edition is limited to 300 copies.
Copy number

176